Sports Superstars

LIONEL MESSI

BY THOMAS K. ADAMSON

BELLWETHER MEDIA • MINNEAPOLIS, MN

Torque brims with excitement perfect for thrill-seekers of all kinds. Discover daring survival skills, explore uncharted worlds, and marvel at mighty engines and extreme sports. In *Torque* books, anything can happen. Are you ready?

This edition first published in 2023 by Bellwether Media, Inc.

No part of this publication may be reproduced in whole or in part without written permission of the publisher. For information regarding permission, write to Bellwether Media, Inc., Attention: Permissions Department, 6012 Blue Circle Drive, Minnetonka, MN 55343.

Library of Congress Cataloging-in-Publication Data

LC record for Lionel Messi available at: https://lccn.loc.gov/2022050061

Text copyright © 2023 by Bellwether Media, Inc. TORQUE and associated logos are trademarks and/or registered trademarks of Bellwether Media, Inc.

Editor: Kieran Downs   Designer: Josh Brink

Printed in the United States of America, North Mankato, MN.

TABLE OF CONTENTS

GOAL-SCORING MACHINE	4
WHO IS LIONEL MESSI?	6
YOUNG TALENT	8
BECOMING A SOCCER SUPERSTAR	12
THE MESSI LEGEND	20
GLOSSARY	22
TO LEARN MORE	23
INDEX	24

GOAL-SCORING MACHINE

FC Barcelona is playing in the 2015 **Copa del Rey** Final. Lionel Messi takes the ball. He moves past one player. Then three **defenders** get in his way. Messi **dribbles** through them with amazing speed.

He cuts to his left past another defender. He fires the ball. The shot is perfect. **Goal** for Messi!

WHO IS LIONEL MESSI?

Many fans say Lionel Messi is the world's greatest soccer player. He is a skilled dribbler and passer. He plays for Paris Saint-Germain and his home country of Argentina. He has also played for FC Barcelona.

Soccer Riches

In 2021-2022, Messi was the highest paid athlete in the world. He made $130 million.

LIONEL MESSI

BIRTHDAY	June 24, 1987
HOMETOWN	Rosario, Argentina
POSITION	striker
HEIGHT	5 feet 7 inches
SIGNED	FC Barcelona on December 14, 2000

He helped Barcelona win **La Liga** 10 times. He scored 672 goals while playing for Barcelona.

7

YOUNG TALENT

Messi was born in Rosario, Argentina. He played soccer with his older brothers and cousins. Even at age 4, he was a great ball handler. He could dribble past other players with ease.

LIONEL MESSI, AGE 1

At age 6, Messi joined the youth program of Rosario's **professional** (pro) soccer team, Newell's Old Boys. Pro teams in other countries noticed Messi's talent, too.

LIONEL MESSI

Messi was small for his age. Doctors did many tests. They found out he was not growing as he should be. He needed expensive shots.

When he was 13, FC Barcelona made him an offer. He agreed to play at their youth **academy**. The team paid his medical costs. Messi's family moved to Spain.

MESSI WITH HIS FAMILY

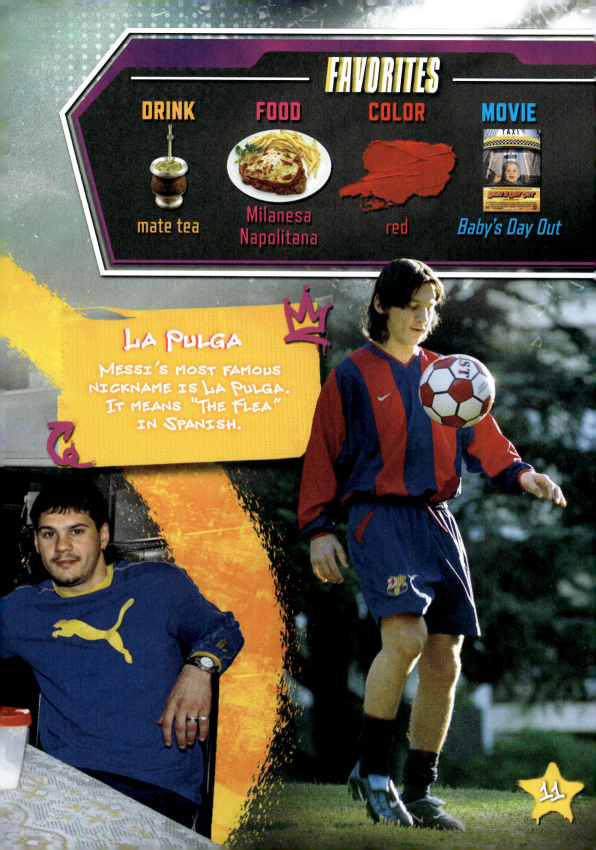

FAVORITES

DRINK — mate tea
FOOD — Milanesa Napolitana
COLOR — red
MOVIE — Baby's Day Out

La Pulga

Messi's most famous nickname is La Pulga. It means "The Flea" in Spanish.

BECOMING A SOCCER SUPERSTAR

Messi first played for Barcelona in 2004 at the age of 17. In 2007, he scored three goals in one game against Real Madrid. The soccer world took notice.

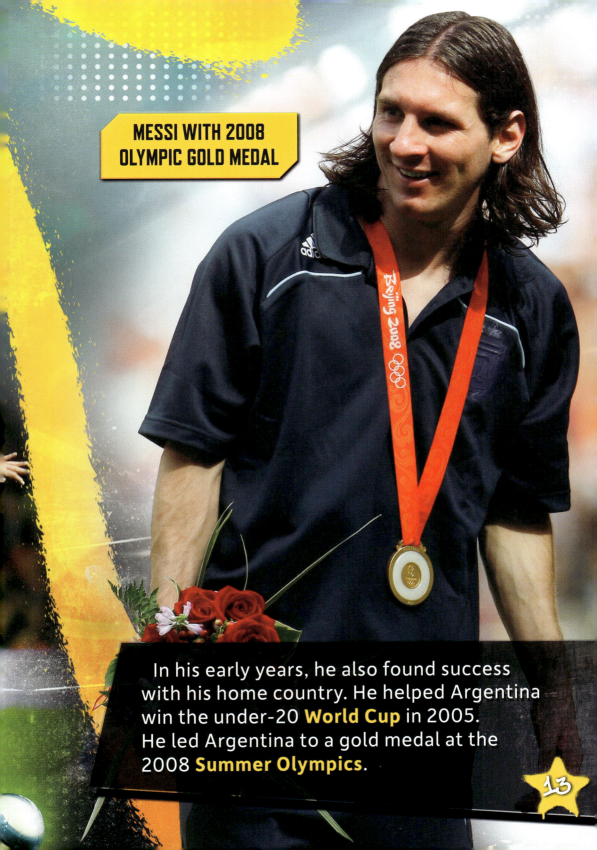

MESSI WITH 2008 OLYMPIC GOLD MEDAL

In his early years, he also found success with his home country. He helped Argentina win the under-20 **World Cup** in 2005. He led Argentina to a gold medal at the 2008 **Summer Olympics**.

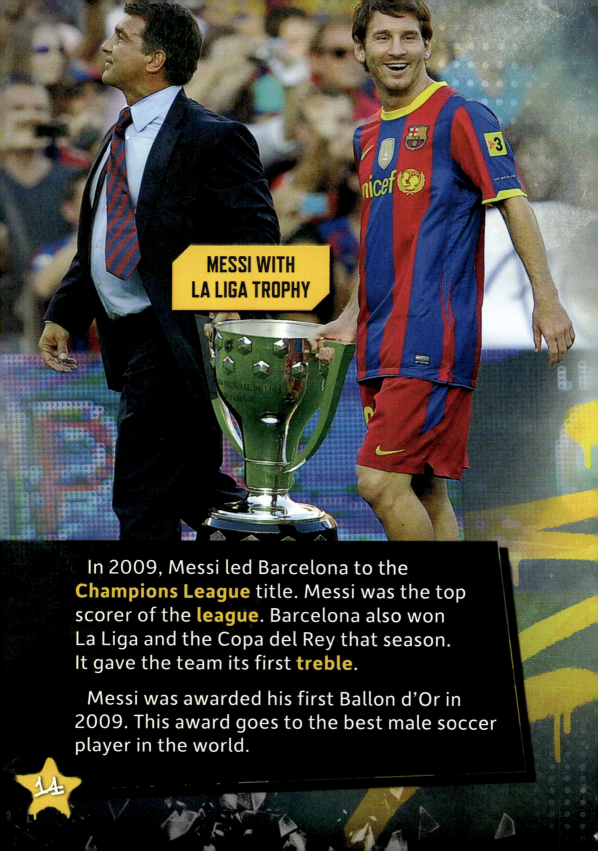

MESSI WITH LA LIGA TROPHY

In 2009, Messi led Barcelona to the **Champions League** title. Messi was the top scorer of the **league**. Barcelona also won La Liga and the Copa del Rey that season. It gave the team its first **treble**.

Messi was awarded his first Ballon d'Or in 2009. This award goes to the best male soccer player in the world.

LIONEL MESSI MAP

- FC Barcelona, Barcelona, Spain — 2004 to 2021
- Argentina National Team, Buenos Aires, Argentina — 2004 to present
- Paris Saint-Germain, Paris, France — 2021 to present

BALLON D'OR AWARD

Messi continued his excellent play. He won three more Ballon d'Or awards. He became the first player to win four in a row!

In 2012, he scored his 233rd goal for Barcelona. That made him the team's all-time leading scorer. In 2014, he became La Liga's leading scorer.

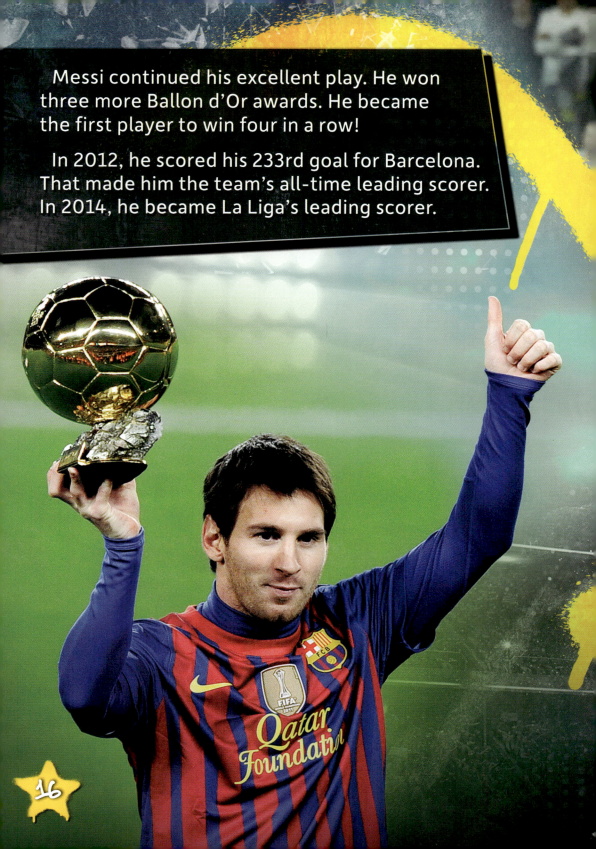

Messi helped Barcelona win La Liga 10 times. The team also won four Champions League titles. They won another treble in the 2014–2015 season.

Messi has led the Argentina National Team in many World Cups. In 2014, he scored 4 goals in the **tournament**. Argentina advanced to the final. But they lost to Germany. Messi won the Golden Ball award as the tournament's best player.

Another Scoring Record

In the 2011–2012 season, Messi set the record for most goals scored in a single season. He scored an amazing 73 goals!

TIMELINE

— 2000 —
Messi agrees to join the FC Barcelona youth program

— 2004 —
Messi plays his first game for FC Barcelona

— 2007 —
Messi scores three goals in one game against Real Madrid

2014 WORLD CUP FINAL

— 2009 —
Messi wins his first Ballon d'Or award for the best player in soccer

— 2021 —
French club Paris Saint-Germain announces signing Messi

THE MESSI LEGEND

Messi continues to be a soccer powerhouse. He won a record seventh Ballon d'Or in 2021.

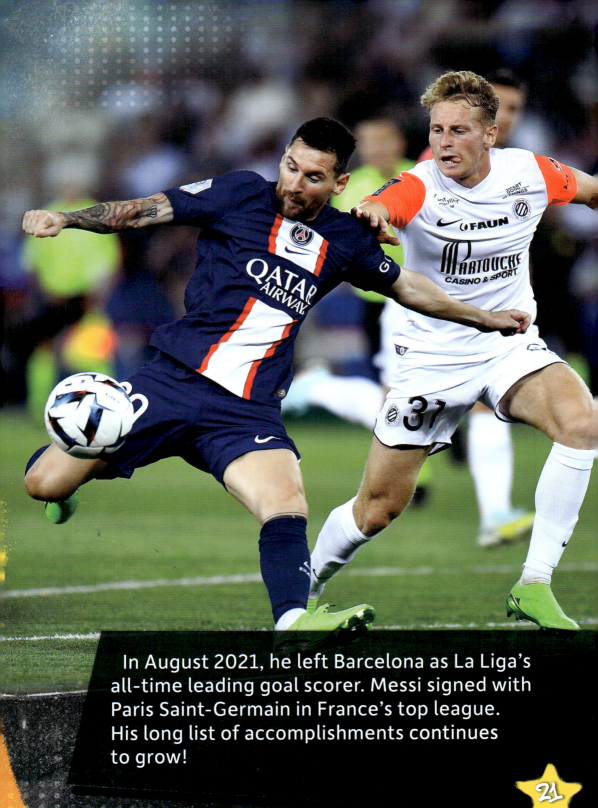

In August 2021, he left Barcelona as La Liga's all-time leading goal scorer. Messi signed with Paris Saint-Germain in France's top league. His long list of accomplishments continues to grow!

GLOSSARY

academy—a school that teaches a certain subject

Champions League—a European soccer tournament where the winners of top European leagues play each other to decide the best team in Europe

Copa del Rey—the championship tournament for professional soccer in Spain

defenders—players who try to stop the player with the ball from advancing or scoring

dribbles—controls the soccer ball with the feet while moving

goal—a score in soccer; a player scores a goal by sending the ball into the other team's net.

La Liga—Spain's top men's soccer league

league—a large group of sports teams that often play each other

professional—related to a player or team that makes money playing a sport

Summer Olympics—a worldwide summer sports contest held in a different country every four years

tournament—a series of games in which several teams try to win the championship

treble—an event in which a team wins three major European titles in one season

World Cup—an international soccer competition held every four years; the World Cup is the world's largest soccer tournament.

TO LEARN MORE

AT THE LIBRARY

Kerry, Isaac. *What You Never Knew about Lionel Messi*. North Mankato, Minn.: Capstone, 2023.

Savage, Jeff. *FC Barcelona: Soccer Champions*. Minneapolis, Minn.: Lerner Publications, 2019.

Stabler, David. *Meet Lionel Messi*. Minneapolis, Minn.: Lerner Publications Company, 2022.

ON THE WEB

Factsurfer.com gives you a safe, fun way to find more information.

1. Go to www.factsurfer.com

2. Enter "Lionel Messi" into the search box and click 🔍.

3. Select your book cover to see a list of related content.

INDEX

Argentina, 6, 8, 13, 18
awards, 13, 14, 15, 16, 17, 18, 20
Ballon d'Or, 14, 15, 16, 20
Champions League, 14, 18
childhood, 8, 9, 10, 12, 13
Copa del Rey, 4, 14
family, 8, 10
favorites, 11
FC Barcelona, 4, 6, 7, 10, 12, 14, 16, 18, 21
France, 21
goal, 4, 7, 12, 16, 18, 21
gold medal, 13
Golden Ball award, 18
La Liga, 7, 14, 16, 18, 21

map, 15
Newell's Old Boys, 9
nickname, 11
Paris Saint-Germain, 6, 21
profile, 7
records, 16, 18, 20, 21
Rosario, 8, 9
Spain, 10
Summer Olympics, 13
timeline, 18–19
tournament, 18
treble, 14, 18
trophy shelf, 17
World Cup, 13, 18, 19

The images in this book are reproduced through the courtesy of: Visionhaus/ Getty Images, front cover (hero); Ververidis Vasilis, p. 3 (Messi); DPPI Media/ Alamy, p. 4; David Ramos/ Getty Images, pp. 4-5 (game); A. Taoualit, pp. 6-7; donfiore, p. 7 (flag); Christian Bertrand, pp. 7, 23; ARCHIVO GBB/ Alamy, p. 8; ZUMA/ Alamy, p. 9; El Grafico/ Getty Images, pp. 10, 11; Alexandr Vorobev, p. 11 (drink); bonchan, p. 11 (food); Elena11, p. 11 (color); Dominicbillings/ Wiki Commons, p. 11 (movie); CESAR RANGEL/ Stringer/ Getty Images, p. 12; Stu Forster/ Staff/ Getty Images, p. 13; JOSEP LAGO/ Stringer/ Getty Images, p. 14; Denis Doyle/ Stringer/ Getty Images, pp. 15, 18 (2007); PhotoLondonUK, p. 15 (Paris, France); BearFotos, p. 15 (Barcelona, Spain); Adwo, p. 15 (Buenos Aires, Argentina); LLUIS GENE/ Getty Images, p. 16; NurPhoto/ Getty Images, pp. 17, 19 (2021); Kyodo/ AP Images, pp. 18-19 (game); Ank Kumar/ Wiki Commons, p. 19 (2009); Xavier Laine/ Getty Images, p. 20: Aurelien Meunier - PSG/ Getty Images, p. 21.